PURCHASING PERFORMANCE MEASUREMENTS:
A ROADMAP FOR EXCELLENCE

Mel Pilachowski

PT Publications, Inc.
3109 45th Street, Suite 100
West Palm Beach, FL 33407-1915

Library of Congress Cataloging in Publication Data

Pilachowski, Mel, 1946-
Purchasing performance measurements: a roadmap for excellence/Mel Pilachowski
          p.   cm.
      Includes index.
      ISBN 0-945456-21-2 (trade paperback)
1. Industrial procurement—Evaluation. 2. Industrial procurement—Quality Control. 3. Performance standards. 4. Benchmarking (Management) I. Title.
HD39.5.P55   1996
658.7'2—dc20   95-49424
                                                    CIP

TABLE OF CONTENTS

PREFACE

The metrics used in traditional purchasing are often just a variation of monitoring receipts. Traditional metrics concentrate on labor productivity and ignore true cost drivers such as product design complexity, process complexity, excessive lead time (time-based competition), quality problems, space utilization, manufacturing flexibility and set-ups. As you can see, metrics must be closely tied to the modern-day virtues of agility and leanness. The aim of the new metrics is to begin and continue the process of reducing both cost and cycle times. There are a number of lessons to be learned from this shift.

Foremost is the lesson that if you can't measure something, then you won't be able to manage it. Measurement is important because people respect what you measure and attempt to do their best. In other words, what gets measured, gets done. Measurements are also useful for motivating people, far more effective, we feel, than slogans on coffee mugs. People do as they are measured. If you want to change behavior, change the measurement. We have also found that people want to excel when given a chance. At our clients, we have found that when they measure everybody for their achievement toward company-wide goals, then people begin to make excellence a way of life in their jobs.

Another important factor which we cannot forget is that the customer, whether internal or external, is your ultimate judge of product or service performance. All measurements must point toward the goals of total customer satisfaction and meeting customer requirements. Metrics should reflect the time it takes to respond to changing customer demands. At the same time, however, you cannot sacrifice flexibility, efficiency, effectiveness and the attainment of Six Sigma quality levels for products/ services, processes, data, and time.

Time is the central component of all new metrics which serve the aims of purchasing performance. Peter Drucker says that time is becoming the new corporate metric. It is becoming the equivalent of cost and quality as time-to-market emerges as the critical factor of the future. Furthermore, the time you take to incorporate changes in your processes and systems will determine whether you are able to compete at the world class level.

There are many different kinds of measurements. Which ones you use will be determined by the nature of your business. In *World Class: Measuring Its Achievement* (ISBN: 0-945456-05-0; PT Publications, Inc.,

West Palm Beach, FL), we have attempted to put all of the different categories in one book which tells the value of measurement for each. *Supplier Certification II: A Handbook for Achieving Excellence Through Continuous Improvement* (ISBN: 0-945456-08-5; PT Publications, Inc., West Palm Beach, FL) also contains a discussion of performance measurements.

Measurement Principles

Whatever metrics you decide will work best in your organization, there are certain principles which should not be avoided. Outstanding among these principles is the necessity of sitting down with your suppliers and getting them involved in the development of meaningful measurements. They will be far less effective if both sides don't agree to the usefulness of the measurement system. Besides meaningful, all measurements should be fair, easy to administer and nonsubjective with little calibration error. You should also select the fewest possible number of parameters without diminishing the objectives of the measurement. Too many parameters often lead to little or no action. Lastly, the cost of maintaining any measurements you develop should be one order of magnitude lower than the tangible benefits to be derived.

All of the measurements we discuss in this book serve to reinforce your company's strategy. We believe that tracking and measurements must be followed to ensure that each element of that strategy is being properly implemented. It is the obligation of everybody in your company to determine what measurements should be utilized and how they will be maintained.

One of the most effective means of improving purchasing performance is to use benchmarking to elevate both your company and your suppliers to world class levels. When Motorola wanted to revamp its order processing system, for example, they studied the operations at Land's End. American Express was studied for its billing systems, TRW for internal audit and payroll, as well as Sears, Penney's, Wards and L.L. Bean for other operations.

Once you have found out what world class companies do, then it becomes a matter of ensuring that your organization stays the course. This is done with appropriate measurements. It's a job that must be done and we aim to show you how in this book.

Peter L. Grieco, Jr.
President and CEO, Pro-Tech
West Palm Beach, FL

HOW TO USE THIS BOOK

This book is designed to be used in conjunction with the corollary texts in our Purchasing Series. Please call us at the number below for more information about utilizing our tools. The idea behind this book is to read it with a pen in your hand so that you can answer the questions and write down the plans you are going to put into action. For those people who use this book alone, there is enough information to get you started on the road to excellence. Remember, however, that roadmaps such as this book are best accompanied by travel guides such as the ones we offer in the field of purchasing. Together, they can make your journey a rewarding one.

HELP DESK HOTLINE
1-800-547-4326

In order to answer the questions of our readers, we have established a Help Desk Hotline at our corporate headquarters in West Palm Beach, Florida. We invite you to call us with your queries about how to use the forms and tools in this book.

We also invite you to use our HELP DESK HOTLINE to find out more about other books we publish, as well as our *Supplier Surveys and Audits Forms* software and a videotape series entitled **Supplier Certification: The Path to Excellence**. In addition to books, software and videotapes, we offer over 80 courses which can be scheduled for intensive, in-house seminars. Call us for details.

INTRODUCTION

CHAPTER ONE

In today's highly competitive marketplace, companies must explore every opportunity to improve their competitive advantage. Continuous improvement is the key to success in this environment. In order to make substantial progress on the road to improvement, we must first measure and take stock of where we are. Purchasing Performance Measurements provide us with this information by establishing:

a benchmark,
a baseline,
a current status, and
a starting point.

We can then identify both the strong and weak points of the business and develop action plans for improvement. With clearly defined goals/objectives in mind, we can use Purchasing Performance Measurements to track improvement and to identify areas requiring corrective action. Measurements allow us to focus all areas of the business on the "action plan."

WHY MEASURE PERFORMANCE?

The answer to that question is simple. We measure performance in order to:

Maintain the Competitive Edge.

Maintain our progress toward institutionalizing the Continuous Improvement Process (CIP).

Achieve World Class purchasing performance.

Based upon your business experience, review the major reasons for the development and utilization of Performance Measurements.

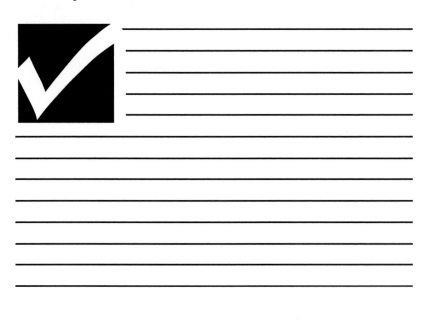

WHY DO INITIATIVES STALL?
OR FAIL?

There are a number of reasons why Performance Measurement initiatives stall and/or fail. But the number one reason is:

MANAGEMENT

All too often, management does not do the job they are supposed to do. That job is to:

Determine the objectives of an organization and then guide the people and other resources in the successful achievement of those objectives.

You can keep on track with your initiative by keeping the following performance questions in mind:

What is performance?
What is performing?   What is not performing?
What is the action required?
What is the follow-up action?
What is the benchmark?
When will it be done?
Who is responsible?

MANAGEMENT OF RESOURCES

Measuring Operational Efficiency — Performance Management

We have learned from our Far Eastern competitors that all resources are critical to peak operating efficiency. Waste in any form will make us less competitive. Thus, the measurement of efficiency is critical to the viability of the business.

Establishing the Baseline

The move to performance measurement begins with establishing a baseline. If we don't establish an initial baseline of measurement data, it becomes increasingly difficult to measure/identify "real" progress. We have no starting line or basis for developing an improvement program. Improve what? Better than what? etc.

Capturing, Summarizing and Evaluating Data

Who should be responsible? Do we need a specialized audit team for measuring performance? In order to be meaningful and provide a catalyst for positive change, data should be collected, summarized and evaluated by the people responsible for the activity being measured. Management reports are a useful means of communication and a good progress monitoring tool. However, corrective action should take place at the source. For example, by an operator at a machine or data entry operator at the source.

Identifying Opportunities

What should you correct or improve? Where should you improve? These are the two basic questions which must be answered by an effective Performance Measurement program. More about this later.

"Cloning" Success

"Clone" your success stories. Successful operations should be modeled and implemented in other areas of the business. Use our Management Cycle on the next page to provide you with a visual reminder of what is necessary. In the next chapter, we will begin our discussion of implementation.

MANAGEMENT CYCLE

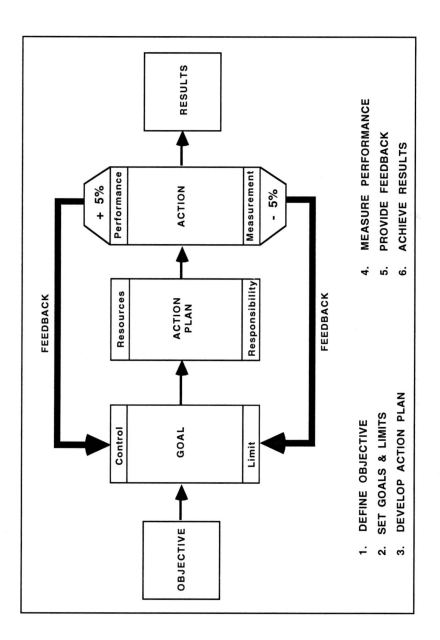

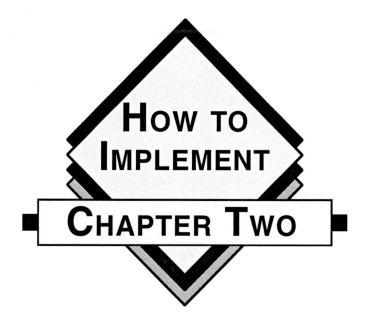

How to Implement

Chapter Two

The gathering and analyzing of purchasing performance data is essential. And it is also essential that both should be based upon the scientific method, that is, the unbiased evaluation of actual capabilities and capacities. In many companies, we find that the problem is not collecting data. Most organizations gather a wealth of data, but the bulk of it is never used in a scientific way. It is never used for problem identification and the development of corrective actions which continuously improve the process or product. Most of the data just sits on the shelf gathering dust. In our process, this performance data is used to identify the root causes of problems and then to identify the most cost-effective approach which will resolve the issue. That is the secret of continuous improvement and it relies on the collection of accurate data.

The gathering of accurate data requires a lot of hard work. The acquisition of data, its evaluation and the launching of the corrective action cycle is typically an eight- to twelve-month cycle. It has to be this long in order to ensure that you will be able to provide 100% quality, 100% count accuracy and 100% on-time delivery. The 100% level is only obtainable when all the required processes are under control and you will know that only if you are measuring performance on a continuous basis.

How, then, will we know if we are succeeding? We measure purchasing performance in order to be predictable, so that we know where we have been, where we are and where we are going. Today, we must use new yardsticks which provide information to make decisions. Then, we will be able to compare actual data against predicted performance. This gives us the opportunity to take corrective action, to be proactive, to measure the predictability of the outcomes of decision-making in real time.

This is best accomplished through a system of measurement that reflects a Total Business Concept. In general, the use of TBC measurements will show:

1. **How close we are to having on-line, real-time information about Purchasing activities. Current information coupled with supplier involvement will provide a new approach.**

2. **How accurate our information is. We all know that a small mistake compounds over time. Unlike interest on your personal investments, this is not favorable. The surveyor who makes a mistake of one degree can cost you many valuable acres of land.**

3. **How much nonvalue-added activity is present in Purchasing. Waste, today, is too often accepted as a given and absorbed into overhead costs. This is truly a reactive way of thinking and must change as we compete in a world market.**

4. **How actual performance compares to the stated plan. Observing this variance is instrumental in making new plans which take corrective action. Those who don't learn from the mistakes of the past are doomed to repeat them.**

These new yardsticks are, in essence, measuring the performance of the whole company. Our principal thrust should be to emphasize a total cost-oriented, rather than a price-oriented, approach in the implementation of purchasing performance measurements.

What steps should be employed in developing and implementing a successful Purchasing Performance Measurement Program

Define Criteria and Responsibility
What will be measured? ————————————————

How?————————————————————

Reporting vehicle? ——————————————————

What should the responsible employee/function do? ————

Establish Goals and Objectives
What are we trying to accomplish? ——————————

Why?————————————————————————

Benefits? ———————————————————————

How will you attain them? ——————————————

How will we know when we get there? ————————

Implement Benchmarking
What are best-in-class performance levels?————————

Gap identification? ——————————————————

Cycle time reporting? ————————————————

Who will provide data? ————————————————

Which companies can contribute? ———————————

Where will you obtain consulting assistance?————————

Measure and Monitor Performance
Reporting cycles must be established. Who will monitor?————

Progress?———————————————————————

Performance?—————————————————————

Timetables? —————————————————————

Review Results and Required Actions
What levels are involved?————————————————

Top management? ——————————————————

What are the intermediate milestones?—————————

Determine Corrective Action Required
Policy(s)? ——————————————————————

Procedural? —————————————————————

Ongoing development? ————————————————

Who is responsible?——————————————————

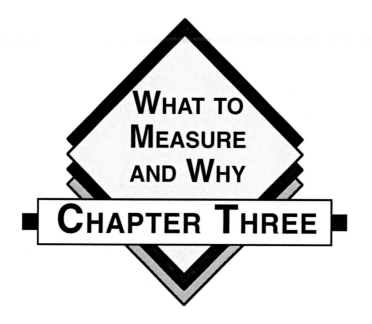

WHAT TO MEASURE AND WHY

CHAPTER THREE

One of the hardest tasks facing a company is establishing meaningful measurements. Take a look at your current measurements. How many of your current measurements complement and interface with each other? For example, do you measure Purchase Price Variance (PPV) while the competition measures Acquisition Cost or Cost of Procurement? If this is the case, while you are driving prices down, the cost of manufacturing is rocketing upward. This is one of many examples of measurement conflicts in a company.

You must be sure that all measurements are interrelated. The key is to establish a benchmark today with goals and objectives which must be accomplished. Once a baseline is established, you should measure and monitor your progress toward the goal. Perhaps most importantly, measurements are useful as a dynamic management tool which establishes a results orientation in the workplace.

Companies make forecasts and set schedules based on these forecasts. As actual sales materialize, a discrepancy develops between the forecasted and the actual. This varying demand requires Purchasing to change the supply process and causes products to move ahead of schedule and some to be delayed or cancelled entirely. Forecasts are developed from the best information available at the time. But, after the forecast is made, things begin to happen—emergency breakdowns, unexpected shortages, and changes in demand. Internally, we face engineering changes, material substitutions, late deliveries, scrap, rework, inventory errors, quality and tooling problems, inoperative machines, absenteeism, paper-work errors and changes in the delivery schedule.

The ability of an organization to measure is the key to success. Consequently, the organization finds itself in the middle of an ever more confusing state where due dates are not met and where there is more work-in-process, raw material and finished inventory than necessary. With the confusion comes frustration, since people want to do their jobs well but are unable to because there is no organized structure. In other words, a lot can and will happen. But, we must move away from being reactive to being proactive. And proactive means sound purchasing performance measurement.

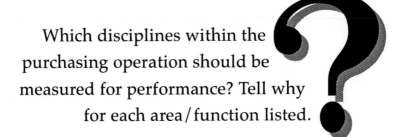

Which disciplines within the purchasing operation should be measured for performance? Tell why for each area/function listed.

ACTIVITY?

_____

_____

_____

_____

WHY?

_____

_____

_____

_____

PERFORMANCE MEASUREMENT INDEX

BUSINESS PLANNING

  1   Business Plan Performance (Actual to Plan)

  2   Sales (Actual to Plan)

  3   Production (Actual to Plan)

  4   Master Production Schedule Attainment

  5   Strategic Procurement Planning

OPERATIONAL PLANNING

  6   Material Requirements Plan (MRP)

  7   Capacity Plan

  8   Inventory Control/Cycle Count Program

  9   Purchased Component Inventory Plan

  10   Bill of Material Accuracy

OPERATIONAL PERFORMANCE

  11   Customer Service/Delivery Performance

BUSINESS PLANNING

1. Business Plan Performance (Actual to Plan)

It is critical to evaluate the revenue generation performance of the business as compared to the plan on a month-to-month, quarter-to-quarter, year-to-year basis. The yearly business plan should be used as the baseline for Purchasing measurements. Any revisions to the original plan or "rolling" forecasts of monthly/quarterly performances should be tracked/measured separately.

Source:

CFO
(Chief Financial Officer)

 **Business Plan Performance Measurement Criteria**

The following are acceptable measurement criteria for determining the performance accuracy of the business plan. All or some of the criteria should be evaluated. Additional "localized" criteria may be substituted where applicable.

- **Income, stated in dollars ($) against budgeted business plan dollars ($).**

- **Return on Investment (ROI), stated as a percentage (%) against budgeted business plan.**

- **Return on Net Assets (RONA), stated as a percentage (%) against budgeted business plan.**

- **Earnings Before Interest and Taxes (EBIT).**

2. Sales (Actual to Plan)

This performance measurement is a key indicator of both the "health" of the sales/shipment effort and the accuracy/predictability of the sales forecast/plan as it relates to Purchasing. The figures outlined in the yearly business plan should be used as the baseline for measurement. In addition, any business plan revisions and/or short-term forecasts should be tracked separately.

Source: Marketing
Finance
Materials

Sales and Marketing Performance Measurement Criteria

The following are acceptable criteria for measuring sales plan performance:

- **Stated in terms of actual dollars ($) of sales by month against budgeted business plan dollars ($).**

- **Stated in units of actual shipments/sales by month against plan.**

- **Order input, in dollars and/or units, against plan.**

- **Actual backlog, in dollars and/or units, against plan.**

- **Actual finished goods inventory level against plan, in dollars ($) and/or units.**

- **Actual backlog levels against plan in dollars ($).**

- **Cycle time of order processing.**

- **Level loading of requirements.**

3. Production Plan (Actual to Plan)

In order to support the sales plan with supplier on-time delivery, it is essential to establish an overall production plan. Hopefully, this can be done by discrete product lines which will drive the business planning process. This plan will form the basis for a review of capacity and manpower constraints, etc. All performance measurements should be based on actual monthly results from the documented production plan of the overall budgeted business plan.

Source:

Materials
Finance

 **Production Plan**
Measurement Criteria

The following are acceptable criteria for measuring production plan performance:

- **Actual production rate, in dollars ($) and/or units against the production plan. A detailed breakdown by product lines provides a meaningful trend indicator/ management tool, if obtainable.**

- **The production plan equal to the sales plan, plus or minus the "planned" increases or decreases in inventory levels and backlog.**

4. (MPS) Master Production Schedule Attainment

In order to ensure the integrity of Purchasing, the effectiveness of the master production schedule (MPS) is critical to developing meaningful performance measurements centered on schedule attainment. Frozen time fences must be maintained or shifting priorities will reduce the schedule to a series of shifting expedite "hot" lists.

Source:
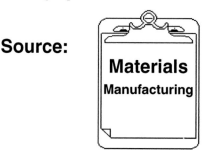

Materials

Manufacturing

 ### Master Production Schedule (MPS) Measurement Criteria

Generally, historical comparative data should be collected and documented on a fiscal month basis. Graphic representations of the statistics should be prominently displayed and utilized as a performance measurement for the responsible functional areas (production / manufacturing materials, etc.). Acceptable variance to plan criteria (2% over or under plan) must be included in the performance measurement procedure.

Attainment should be measured in one or all of the following areas:

- **Actual vs. scheduled completion dates**

- **Actual units vs. plan**

- **Actual dollars vs. plan**

OPERATIONAL PLANNING

5. Strategic Procurement Planning

Briefly, these are the steps a company needs to take to develop a supply management strategy based on understanding your market and level of risk:

- **Determine influences on company results.**
  - **Determine market success elements.**
  - **Weight elements relative to market success.**
  - **Calculate index of influence on company result.**
- **Calculate procurement risk.**
  - **Determine relative strength of competitive forces.**
    - **Bargaining power**
    - **Rivalry**
    - **Substitution**
    - **Entry barriers**
  - **Position material on matrix.**
- **Select appropriate strategy.**

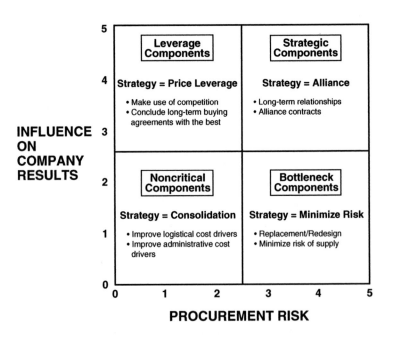

6. Material Requirements Plan (MRP)

This measurement is designed to evaluate the performance of the material requirements planning system/activity. A measurement of the reliability of material availability is critical at all levels of the planning/production process.

Source: **Materials**
Purchasing
Manufacturing

 **Materials Requirements Planning Measurement Criteria**

The following are acceptable criteria for measuring MRP performance. Where data is available, a combination of measurements is recommended.

- **On-time (to schedule completion dates) measured against total released orders.**

- **Orders with 100% material availability measured against total released orders.**

- **Orders with current start/completion dates measured against total released orders. (A measure of total production performance and effective system maintenance — orders closed on-time, etc.)**

_____

_____

_____

_____

_____

7. Capacity Requirements Plan (CRP)

The measurement of Capacity Requirements Planning utilization ensures that a comprehensive review of capacity requirements is an integral part of the business planning process and is a cohesive portion of ongoing plant/company operational planning. Continual measurement allows for a dynamic test of viability of the capacity plan. It allows us to plan supplier capacity in conjunction with internal capacity requirements.

Source:  **Materials**
Manufacturing

 ### Capacity Requirements Plan (CRP) Measurement Criteria

The following are acceptable criteria for measuring CRP performance:

- **Master schedule generated capacity requirements against available machine and manpower capacity (load vs. capacity).**

- **Released hours against the (time released) capacity plan.**

- **Actual against planned idle capacity for contingency (both machine and manpower).**

_____

_____

_____

_____

_____

8. Inventory Control/Cycle Count Program

A cycle counting program is designed to maintain the high level of inventory accuracy required by a totally integrated manufacturing system. The program is based upon physical inventory techniques — performing counts/reconciliations on a continuous basis. Items are counted on a frequency (cycle) consistent with their importance to the purchasing and manufacturing processes and their propensity for error.

Source:

Materials
Purchasing

 **Inventory Accuracy/Cycle Count Measurement Criteria**

• **Consistent inventory management.**

• **The number of accurate/correct counted items (both in quantity and location) against the total number selected for counting.**

Graphic displays of the results should be prominently displayed in the manufacturing/warehouse facility, as a constant reminder of record accuracy/performance measurement.

Note: A Pareto chart on the causes of errors should also be prominently displayed.

_____

_____

_____

_____

9. Purchased Component Inventory Plan

This monthly measurement is intended to track actual performance of purchased components within inventory segments and total inventory against budgeted / forecast inventory investment. The performance measurement is expressed as a percentage (%) of actual to budgeted. At the end of the month, the measurement is plotted on a performance grid and graphic display. We should track this by each purchasing professional buyer or by commodity.

Source:

**Finance
Materials
Purchasing**

 **Inventory Plan
Measurement Criteria**

The following are acceptable criteria for measurement of purchased component inventory planning accuracy / reliability:

- **Actual dollars ($) of purchased inventory, (investment), in total and by inventory bucket (finished goods, work-in-process and raw materials), against the budgeted inventory plan.**

- **Actual inventory turns against budgeted inventory turns.**

- **Actual days of inventory against plan/target.**

- **Reduction in supplier inventory levels.**

- **JIT inventory performance.**

10. Bill of Material (BOM) Accuracy

There needs to be an ongoing review of the contents of the BOM as used in the company vs. the drawing and/or what appears in computer files. As the cornerstone of the "recipe," bills of material must be maintained at a 99% plus accuracy level. Material requirements planning explosion, purchasing requirement, kit requisitioning, product cost roll-up/build-up, etc. are all dependent upon documented bills of material/product structures.

Source:

Engineering
/Product
Development
Purchasing

 **Bill of Material (BOM) Measurement Criteria**

A comprehensive, ongoing program of review must be maintained and can be linked to purchased components selected. All results should be quantified and graphically displayed. The following are measurements which should be considered in developing the program:

- **Accuracy of purchased components, forms, parts, quantities, etc. at all levels of the bills.**

- **Actual against planned effectivity dates.**

- **Obsolete purchased inventory (based on phase-out/ phase-in programs) as a percentage (%) of total inventory.**

_____

_____

_____

_____

_____

OPERATIONAL PERFORMANCE

11. Customer Service/Delivery Performance

This measurement, which is perhaps the best indication of overall operational performance, reflects actual delivery performance to the stated delivery "promise." Both Purchasing and each supplier contribute to the success of the customer. While a difference of opinion exists as to the relative importance of customer request dates and published lead time delivery rates, etc., it is the original "promise date" which is the foundation of excellent customer service. It is derived through careful evaluation of the customer's needs/requests and the manufacturing firm's capabilities and is the basis for the company's credibility in the marketplace. It is critical that this "promise date" be reflected as the system's due/completion date and utilized as a performance baseline.

Source:
Marketing
Customer
Service
Purchasing

 ### Customer Service
Measurement Criteria

The following are acceptable alternative and/or compatible measurement criteria for measuring customer service/delivery performance.

- **Actual completed orders to "promised" delivery date, stated as a percentage (%).**

- **Actual line items shipped against total committed line items, to promised delivery date.**

- **Actual dollars ($) shipped, "on-time," against total "promised"/committed dollars ($).**

- **Total past due shipments, in dollars ($), orders and/or line items compared to previous performance by month.**

PURCHASING PERFORMANCE

Up to this point, we have reviewed the interrelationship of performance measurements to the business organization as a total entity. Now, let's turn our attention to the main focus of this book — Purchasing Performance Measurements.

A purchasing executive cannot wait for problems. He or she must review what the plant community needs and communicate those desires to the supplier base in a manner which avoids expediting, firefighting and other wasteful activities. In addition, Purchasing must be aware of both manufacturing and marketing requirements in order to satisfy customers' demands. In order to be on top of the situation, accurate information is a necessity.

Purchasing has a unique opportunity and obligation to initiate purchasing measurements, but it cannot succeed alone. Previously, we have showed how Purchasing will work with Finance in the establishment of new yardsticks based on total cost. This relationship must continue in the area of performance measurement as well. Certainly, Engineering, Quality and Manufacturing have a large role to play, too. Purchasing must not think its responsibility begins with a request to buy and ends when the material or service reaches requisition or the receiving room door. Keep in mind the changing role of Purchasing which is better defined as Procurement and Materials Management. Purchasing's responsibility begins with the birth of an idea for a new product or service, follows it through its development in Design, its future plans in Marketing, its construction in Manufacturing and its eventual "leaving of the nest" in Sales and ends once any field failures are resolved. To satisfy the customer is why Purchasing measures performance.

Another responsibility of Purchasing is to measure its own performance. This does not mean only measuring the performance of the buyer or the ability to ensure on-time delivery, but also measuring how well it satisfies the rest of the company.

Performance measurement is a difficult job which, because of the relative importance of purchased material, makes it all the more critical for Purchasing to lead the company. But, as we stated above, it cannot be done alone. Thomas Peters in his book, *Thriving on Chaos*, states that today we need flexibility every bit as much as we need excellence. American business people and decision makers must be shaken up. "What is needed," he insists, "is intelligence, energy, heroic efforts and a renewed emphasis on quality products and performance." This is what teamwork is all about — getting people to appraise your performance so you can see if the outcome you predicted coincides with the state of the real world.

PURCHASING PERFORMANCE MEASUREMENT INDEX

The list that follows is an index to the purchasing performance measurements in this book. They have been grouped into chapters which highlight particular areas of purchasing.

OVERALL MEASUREMENTS

QUALITY MEASUREMENTS

SUPPLY MANAGEMENT MEASUREMENTS

ADMINISTRATIVE MEASUREMENTS

ADDITIONAL MEASUREMENTS

OVERALL MEASUREMENTS

CHAPTER FOUR

The dominant theme in our discussion on purchasing performance is the interrelationship of measurements. By measuring one area in a world class environment, you are in effect measuring how well the whole of your company is working. Quality, for example, is also measured by on-time delivery. You can't have an on-time delivery if there are defective parts in the shipment. As another example, let's consider the time it takes to process purchasing change orders. Surely, this indicates how well your company system performs, but it also tests how well your relationship with suppliers is working.

Purchasing performance indicators should show the existence of proactive thought. They have a theoretical foundation which is remarkably close to the premises underlying the formulation of chaos theory, which is interested in sensitive dependence upon initial conditions. One of the theory's central premises, called the paradox of the butterfly's wings, states that it is impossible to make precise long-range weather forecasts. For a system as complicated as the weather, there is no way for us to take enough measurements to describe current conditions. Hence, we are never sure if the beating of a butterfly's wings in Connecticut will cause a wind storm in southern England.

While we may never know if the whisper of wind around a butterfly grows into a hurricane, we do know that small deviations at Receiving can escalate into major difficulties in Manufacturing and Shipping. By using purchasing performance measurements, we can detect these deviations and avoid "stormy weather." Since small initial differences can lead to huge resulting differences, accurate measurement is so essential. A small deviation can make a huge difference. Measuring those small deviations and taking corrective action are what performance measurements are all about.

The measurements in this chapter are involved in taking a snapshot of activities affecting the purchasing process. World Class purchasing demands interdisciplinary cooperation. This is primarily due to the precision required in scheduling frequent, small deliveries and by the absence of excess inventories which puts a demand on defect-free parts. Thus, Purchasing must operate in an environment in which there is little room for wasteful mistakes. This necessitates gathering input from a number of departments and people in order to make sound procurement decisions.

THROUGHPUT

 Why is this measurement
so meaningful in today's business
environment?

Throughput measures the total amount of production which has been sold. If you bought enough material and components to build 100 products, built 80, have enough material to build 20 more in queue, and stored 10 units in finished goods inventory, your throughput percentage is 70%. Traditional methods would not detect the 30 units either in production or waiting to be sold. They may indicate that the throughput level is at 80 or even 100%, since there is no material left in the storeroom. But, a world class measurement makes no distinctions (as far as the bottom line goes) between material in a queue or in finished goods. The criteria here is simply how much did you sell. If you are overproducing, this measurement tells you so. It may indicate that you are not building to demand, that your company is still operating in a "push," rather than a "pull," environment.

What percentage of your total purchased inventory has been sold?_____%

INVENTORY TURNOVER RATIO

How many inventory turns do you get a year? _____ # / year.

How many inventory turns is your goal? _____ # / year.

The inventory turnover ratio is the forecasted cost of goods sold over the next 12 months divided by the inventory investment.

$$\text{ITR} = \frac{\textbf{Forecasted Cost of Goods}}{\textbf{Inventory Investment}}$$

The measurement of inventory turns is perhaps the single best method for determining the progress of a world class implementation. Inventory turnovers are something like the Dow Jones Industrial Average in that both act as an overall indicator of the movements of many variables. In the case of the ITR, these variables are associated with lot sizing, inventory management, line balancing and the Theory of One. We can increase inventory turns by planning for only as much material as a work station needs to make one product and by minimizing queues so that a work station has only enough material to make a product in its cycle time.

Most companies today are struggling to achieve three inventory turns a year. This means they carry four months of inventory. The industry average is less than three turns per year.

RETURN ON ASSETS

What is your supplier's Return On Asset utilization? ___%

ROA = Net Profits/Total Assets

This is a financial measurement which is viewed differently in the World Class environment. It is not necessary, indeed harmful, to run a machine even if there is no demand. The reason is that idle time is expensive and that a major asset such as a machine has to pay for itself by producing parts. The fallacy in this reasoning is that it is based on a "push" system of manufacturing which only stockpiles subassemblies or finished goods. Warehousing (nothing more than transportation at zero velocity) costs money. The cost of carrying inventory also costs money.

The two costs probably far exceed the cost of idle time. This is not to say that ROA is a useless measurement. It is very useful, given that we plan well and correctly use World Class management techniques. In that situation, where there is little variance between planned and actual, ROA once again becomes valid.

DISTRIBUTION OF DOLLARS EXPENDED

A useful measurement tool is a pie chart which shows how dollars are expended in the procurement process. Use the suggested categories at the left (develop more of your own, if desired) and then divide the pie and put in the percentages as in the sample below. Visual reminders like this provide your organization with a quick and accurate picture of how money and resources are being used.

Capital Equipment	____%
Direct Material	____%
Indirect	____%
Service	____%
Energy	____%
MRO	____%
Distributors	____%
Security	____%

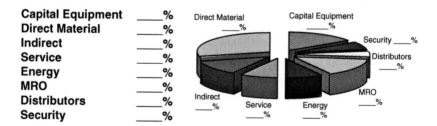

SUPPLIER PERFORMANCE RATING

The Supplier Performance Rating form measures a supplier's performance in six critical areas — certification, product quality, delivery performance, cost performance, cooperation and quantity. The form demonstrates how to quantify performance in each of these areas and use the results to assign a rating. For a further explanation of supplier rating, read Chapter 9 of *Supplier Certification II: A Handbook for Achieving Excellence Through Continuous Improvement* (ISBN 0-945456-08-5; West Palm Beach, FL)

TOTAL VALUATION
Rating Table

Function	Max. Pts.	Earned Pts.
Certification		
Product quality		
Delivery performance		
Cost performance		
Cooperation		
Quantity		
Total	100	

Field failures		
Production downtime		

	Total	

SUPPLIER PERFORMANCE RATING
(PART 1)

CERTIFICATION

Supplier Certification

A supplier nets points for the level of Supplier Certification which it has obtained. The chart below shows the number of points to award a supplier for completion of various phases of the program.

PHASE	MAX. PTS.
Phase One: History and Status	5
Phase Two: Program Review and Process Validation	8
Phase Three: Finalization	13
Phase Four: Certification	20

Field Failures

A supplier with field failures receives negative points when the failures can be proved to be caused by the supplier's components when used within specifications.

Production Downtime

A supplier can also earn negative points in this category when downtime can be proved to be caused by the supplier's components when used within specifications.

SUPPLIER PERFORMANCE RATING
(PART 2)

PRODUCT QUALITY

Goal

Zero-defects to the customer (free from electrical and mechanical failures or defects) and meeting customer requirements.

Material Reject Rate (MRR)

$$MRR = \frac{\text{Total number of rejected incoming and line}}{\text{Total units received}}$$

Legend for MRR:

Excellent	99.8% >	25 points
Good	99.5% < 99.8%	19 points
Satisfactory	99.0% < 99.5%	13 points
Not satisfactory	98.0% < 99.0%	6 points

SUPPLIER PERFORMANCE RATING
(PART 3)

DELIVERY PERFORMANCE

Goal — reduction in cycle time
— keep agreed delivery dates
— short lead times
— quick deliveries for urgent needs
— supply fulfillment in case of market shortages

Valuation Criteria	Score
Material Reject Rate (MRR)	
Lead Times (in relation to competitors) including behavior for urgent needs	
Subsystem Score	

Legend for On-Time Deliveries:

Excellent	99% >		16 points
Good	97% <	99%	12 points
Satisfactory	94% <	97%	8 points
Not satisfactory	90% <	94%	4 points
Not acceptable	<	90%	0 points

Legend for Lead Times:

Excellent	shorter than customer's cycle time	4 points
Good	best of the suppliers of this product	3 points
Satisfactory	equal to market	2 points
Not satisfactory	1 day longer than best	1 point
Not acceptable	2 days longer than best	0 points

SUPPLIER PERFORMANCE RATING (PART 4)

COST PERFORMANCE

Goal — best cost/performance relation

Valuation Criteria	Score
In comparison to other manufacturers and other sources (same product)	
Price Tendency (frequent increases/reductions)	
Subsystem Score	

Cost includes two factors: relative direct cost in comparison to other manufacturers, and relative cost trend in comparison to an industry index.

Scoring:

	Comparison to Competitors	Pts.	Price Tendency	Pts.
Excellent	> 5% lower	15	> 5% below industry index	5
Good	0 < 5% lower	12	2 - 5% below industry index	4
Satisfactory	meets competition	10	±1% industry standard	3
Not satisfactory	0 < 5% higher	7	2 - 5% above industry index	2
Not acceptable	> 5% higher	0	> 5% above industry index	0

SUPPLIER PERFORMANCE RATING
(PART 5)

COOPERATION

Goal — partnership relations

Valuation Criteria	Score
1. Commercial	
2. Technical	
3. Forwarding	
4. Service (after sales)	
Subsystem Score	

Criteria and Scoring for Cooperation

1. Commercial   ___ **points**
— Competence of the internal/external sales organization
— Initiative in case of problems
— Reaction on inquiries
— Information about trends, market fluctuations, technical changes, etc.
— Contract/order processing
— Openness toward cost reduction programs

2. Technical   ___ **points**
— Competence of advisory and support services
— Documentation (quality, completeness, transitions)

3. Forwarding   ___ **points**
— Completeness and quality of shipping documentation (export)
— Reliability of packing
— Completeness and quality of shipping advice notes (import)
— Reliability in meeting shipment deadlines
— Labeling/identification of material

4. Service (after sales)   ___ **points**
— Type, extent and quality of service network
— Quality of services
— Response in case of technical problems
— Fairness

SUPPLIER PERFORMANCE RATING
(PART 6)
QUANTITY

Goal — 100% quantity delivered to order
    — small lot sizes
    — ship to stock

Valuation Criteria	Score
Correct quantity	
Subsystem Score	

Legend for Quantities:

Excellent	99% >	10 points
Good	97% < 99%	7.5 points
Satisfactory	94% < 97%	5.0 points
Not satisfactory	90% < 94%	2.5 points
Not acceptable	< 90%	0 points

The points are based on correct quantity delivered according to schedule or release. Calculations are based on a quarter rating period. The score is calculated from the chart.

INVENTORY CARRYING COST

The following section is divided into two parts. The first part is a form for recording the amounts which you obtain. The second part is a line-by-line description of how to fill in the first part.

I. STORAGE SPACE COSTS   **DOLLARS**
   1. Taxes on land and buildings for stores   _____
   2. Insurance on storage building   _____
   3. Depreciation on storage building   _____
   4. Depreciation on other warehouse installations   _____
   5. Maintenance and repairs of other buildings   _____
   6. Utility costs, including heat, light and water   _____
   7. Janitor, watchman and maintenance salaries   _____
   8. Storage/handling at other locations   _____
      Subtotal: Storage Space   _____

II. HANDLING EQUIPMENT COSTS FOR STORES ONLY
   (not including central trucking)   **DOLLARS**
   9. Depreciation on equipment   _____
   10. Fuel for equipment   _____
   11. Maintenance and repair of equipment   _____
   12. Insurance and taxes on equipment   _____
       Subtotal: Handling Equipment   _____

III. INVENTORY RISK COSTS   **DOLLARS**
   13. Insurance on the inventory   _____
   14. Obsolescence of inventory   _____
   15. Physical deterioration of inventory, incl. scrap   _____
   16. Pilferage   _____
   17. Losses resulting from inventory price declines   _____
       Subtotal: Inventory Risk   _____

IV. TAXES AND SERVICES COSTS   **DOLLARS**
   18. Taxes on inventory   _____
   19. Labor costs of handling and maintaining stock   _____
   20. Clerical costs of keeping records   _____
   21. Employer contributions to Social Security
       for all space, handling and inventory
       service personnel   _____
   22. Unemployment Compensation Insurance for all
       of the above personnel   _____
   23. Employer contributions to pension plans, group
       life, health and accident insurance programs
       for above personnel   _____
   24. A proportionate share of general administration
       overhead, including all taxes, social security,
       pension and employer contributions to insurance
       programs for administrative personnel   _____
       Subtotal: Taxes and Services   _____

V. CAPITAL COSTS   DOLLARS
25. Cost of money   _____
26. Interest on money invested in inventory
     handling and control equipment   _____
27. Interest on money invested in land and
     buildings to store inventory, if owned
     Subtotal: Capital Costs   _____   _____

     GRAND TOTAL: _____

28. Average inventory on hand for storerooms
     considered in the analysis above (in dollars) _____
29. Calculate carrying charge percent by
     dividing #28 into Grand Total Amount   _____%
30. Current cost of money (in percentage)   _____%
31. For TOTAL CHARGE (in percentage), add #29
     to #30   _____%

TOTALS   DOLLARS
   I. STORAGE SPACE COSTS   _____
  II. HANDLING EQUIPMENT COSTS
      FOR STORES ONLY   _____
 III. INVENTORY RISK COSTS   _____
 IV. TAXES AND SERVICES COSTS   _____
  V. CAPITAL COSTS   _____
          TOTAL COSTS   _____

DEVELOPMENT OF INVENTORY CARRYING COSTS

Line No.
1. Estimate of share of real estate taxes paid for the part of the building and land occupied by storage facilities, including inside and outside.
2. Estimate of share of insurance for same areas. NOTE: many large firms are either self-insuring or carrying a large deductible to cover catastrophes only.
3. Annual depreciation actually claimed for the building/land used for stores.
4. Annual depreciation on any other remote locations or temporary locations used for storage.
5. Estimate of annual maintenance costs spent just for storage areas. (If outside, include some snow removal, if appropriate for your area.)
6. Estimate of annual maintenance costs spent just for the storage area buildings.
7. Estimate share of annual expenses for security and janitorial for stores area.
8. Annual costs incurred for storage and handling at other location.
9. Annual depreciation on forklifts, cranes, stackers/pickers, racks, etc. for all equipment used for handling inventory in store area. Do not include any equipment from central trucking, shipping, receiving, operations, etc.
10. Annual estimated fuel costs for above.

11. Estimated annual maintenance costs and/or maintenance contracts for items in #9 above.
12. Annual insurance and taxes on equipment items in No. 9 above, if known.
13. Annual insurance premiums paid to cover casualty losses of stored inventory (not work-in-process), if any.
14. Estimated annual write-offs due to obsolescence. (NOTE: If written off, material must be destroyed and/or disposed of.)
15. Estimated inventory losses due to scrap generated in stores handling, shelf life deterioration, etc. Do not include shop generated scrap or material scrapped as a result of inspection design change.
16. Estimated inventory losses due to employee pilferage for personal use.
17. Estimated reduction of inventory value because of price decline — use the lower of cost or market value.
18. Taxes on inventory are no longer assessed in many states. But when inventory is stored in another state, it would be checked to see if any entry should be made on this line.
19. Labor cost to store inventory. This is the BIG ONE, and should include the annual wages and salaries of all individuals connected with storing inventory. (Do not include material handling such as shipping, receiving, or trucking.)
20. Estimated clerical costs for data entry, cycle counting, reconciliation, error correction, document handling, etc., including time and cost of computer operation, maintenance and reports.
21-24. Fringe benefits. These can be combined and entered into No. 24.
25. Generally thought of as the cost of money. Can be handled in No. 30 as a percentage figure, but not in both places.
26. Estimated cost of interest expense on handling equipment purchases; or, the interest that could have been earned on the money which is tied up in storage handling equipment (related to No. 9 above).
27. Estimated interest cost (either paid or opportunity lost) on the money tied up in storage buildings and land. (Related to No. 3 above.)
28. Since the cost figures developed in the above are annual and apply to the inventory assessment across the year, an average investment-on-hand figure should be determined for the storeroom materials (not WIP or FG).
29. Develop a percentage figure by taking the annual costs (total) over the average investment.
30. Then add the current cost of money, usually thought of as the current prime rate. Sometimes, the actual cost is more or less than the prime, but the prime rate is normally close enough. (DO NOT DUPLICATE line 25 here; it is one or the other.)
31. The total actual current inventory carrying charge is then the sum of line 29 and line 30.

After accumulating all the components of the COI, a carrying cost can be calculated (see lines 28 to 31 above). Use the average inventory value for the areas being considered. It is not necessary, either, to use all inventory to calculate the carrying cost. You can calculate different areas separately in order to emphasize an inventory area in great need of reducing. In fact, the cost of carrying inventory can be used as a tool to convince people throughout the organization that levels must be reduced.

DOLLAR INVENTORY
INVESTMENT BY PLANT

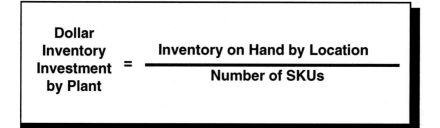

$$\text{Dollar Inventory Investment by Plant} = \frac{\text{Inventory on Hand by Location}}{\text{Number of SKUs}}$$

INVENTORY ACTIVITY

$$\text{Inventory Activity} = \frac{\text{Average Inventory Movement by Plant(s)}}{\text{Total of All Inventory On Hand}}$$

QUALITY MEASUREMENTS

CHAPTER FIVE

Purchasing's thrust in the area of quality is to obtain zero-defect components, material and services from each supplier. Quality is not a nebulous term. At least it shouldn't be. It is a measurable and thus controllable entity.

In Japan, they have a rule called the "40/30/30 rule" which identifies the three major reasons for poor quality. The rule quite simply states that poor design accounts for 40% of quality problems, errors in the manufacturing process account for 30%, and defective parts from suppliers account for the last 30%. In this chapter, we will concentrate on the third percentage area.

Quality, from Purchasing's perspective, mainly centers around the relationships with suppliers in their effort to ensure delivery of zero-defect, or Six Sigma level, products and services to the company. The predominant theme of quality is this: MAKE IT RIGHT THE FIRST TIME. This places an emphasis on defect prevention so that routine inspection is no longer needed. Consequently, the burden of proof will not rest upon inspectors, but on the makers of a part, or suppliers. Quality can not be inspected into a part; it must be designed and produced into the part.

Supplier relations are essential to a successful quality program and developing those relations is the responsibility of Purchasing. What does supplier development mean?

When we say that you should make the supplier a part of your organization for the life of the product and the life of the company, we have specific ideas in mind, not a parental relationship. These ideas are based on the principle that as quality goes up, the cost will inevitably be lower. Sometimes the price goes up.

What are these specific goals and expectations? As a goal, you want suppliers who claim quality ownership... who believe in the zero-defect concept... who maintain the capability to consistently meet the requirements for quality, quantity, cost, and delivery. Here is what you must obtain:

SUPPLIER QUALITY EXPECTATIONS

1.   Quality — conformance to your requirements at all times
2.   Delivery — meeting your scheduled requirements
3.   Quantity — providing the quantity ordered; no more, no less
4.   Cost — reasonable profit margin and low total cost

In addition, you should expect to find the following standards in the supplier's quality process.

QUALITY PROCESS EXPECTATIONS

Supplier quality process should:

1.   Create an improvement environment.
2.   Develop capability to measure quality improvement.
3.   Have short-term goal-setting capabilities to achieve zero-defect standards.
4.   Have long-term goal-setting capabilities to continue zero-defect standards.
5.   Be prevention-oriented rather than approval-oriented.

MEASUREMENTS
FOR RATING
A SUPPLIER'S PERFORMANCE

The first set of measurements is concerned with the level of quality attained by your organization's suppliers.

1. Supplier Quality Rating (SQR) — determined by incoming inspection

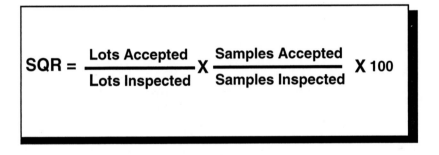

$$SQR = \frac{\text{Lots Accepted}}{\text{Lots Inspected}} \times \frac{\text{Samples Accepted}}{\text{Samples Inspected}} \times 100$$

2. Incoming Parts per Million (IPPM) — determined by incoming inspection

$$IPPM = \frac{\text{Defective Samples}}{\text{Samples Inspected}} \times 1,000,000$$

3.   Supplier Parts per Million (SPPM) — reported by
     each supplier component

$$SPPM = \frac{Defective\ Parts}{Parts\ Used} X\ 1,000,000$$

NUMBER OF DEFECTS

Purpose: This measurement tracks items which are received
                      with defects from suppliers. You should analyze
                      why and what the effect of this measurement is on
                      your company.

Responsibility: The responsibility and authority for supplier perfor-
                      mance and for this measurement should be with
                      Purchasing.

Reporting: The measurements should include graphs which
                      reflect the number, percent and cost of defects. Re-
                      ports should reflect performance by supplier and the
                      total supply base.

Calculation of Defect Dollars:

Dollars = Inspection cost + processing cost + distribution cost

Inspection cost   = Cost of labor to inspect all parts to
                         find bad ones + equipment cost +
                         carrying cost
Processing cost   = Cost of maintaining data and records
                         on defects
Distribution cost = Labor to move it + packing + shipping

REWORK AND SCRAP

Purpose: Both scrap and rework represent waste to World Class efforts. They indicate a supplier's inability to produce a product right the first time. Measurements allow the company to note supplier improvement in reducing this waste.

Responsibility: To determine responsibility, the supplier must first determine why scrap and rework is produced. The causes need to be identified and eliminated by the supplier.

Reporting: Measurements need to be recorded in both reports and graphs. Graphs make visible the severity of the problem and the amount of dollars lost. Reports reflect the opportunity to reduce cost through the elimination of waste.

SCRAP OR REWORK DOLLARS

TIME

REWORK MEASUREMENT CRITERIA

Plot cost per week (materials, labor and overhead).

Formula:
Labor $ to rework + any additional material $ + additional machine $ + overhead $ = total cost for rework

SCRAP MEASUREMENT CRITERIA

Plot cost/week (materials, labor, overhead, and supplies).

Formula:
Material cost for all scrap + machine $ + labor $ + overhead $ added to the point of scrap

QUALITY MEASUREMENTS
ON THE SHOP FLOOR

Why is Statistical Process Control (SPC) a cornerstone of quality?

Deming has advised companies to "make maximum use of statistical knowledge and talent." Why? Because statistical techniques like SPC are the embodiment of the old saying that an ounce of prevention is worth a pound of cure. SPC lets us know when activities are about to deviate outside of control limits and produce a bad part or transaction. This is because statistics allows us to note trends in variances. Once a supplier notices assignable variances, it is then able to make changes which ensure control over quality.

Obviously, if you can predict when a machine will make a bad part or when it needs maintenance, you can reduce rework to negligible levels. All of this also applies to your Supply Management process. The more suppliers enrolled, the less defective material you will receive.

What percentage of your supplier's operations are under the control of Statistical Process Control (SPC)?

$$\frac{\text{\# of supplier critical processes}}{\substack{\text{\# of supplier critical processes} \\ \text{under SPC control at supplier}}} = \%$$

MRB

MRB =   salary and benefit of each functional person
        dedicated to MRB + (Estimated time (hrs. per
        week) each department dedicates to MRB) x
        $50.00

$50.00 is the hourly rate (salary + benefits) for Operating departments

RTV

RTV =   (Freight for return shipment) + (RTV processing
        time (1 hr. @ $50.00)) + (Late delivery cost)

RTV processing time = time spent in Purchasing,
        Accounting, Receiving, QA, and Shipping

COST OF RECEIVING

Cost of receiving = cost to process receipts + material
        movement + storage/inventory cost + cycle
        time cost + cost of processing paperwork

COST OF INSPECTION

Cost of inspection = inspection hours per lot +
        paperwork processing + cost of forms +
        data collection cost + record retention cost +
        handling, storage and movement cost

QUALITY COST INDEX

$$QCI = \frac{\text{Total Purchase Value per Item} + \text{Quality Problem Costs}}{\text{Total Purchase Value per Item}}$$

SUPPLIER QUALITY COST INDEX

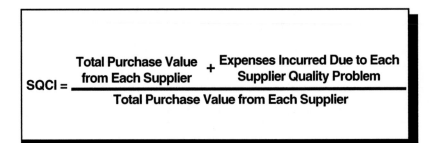

$$SQCI = \frac{\substack{\text{Total Purchase Value} \\ \text{from Each Supplier}} + \substack{\text{Expenses Incurred Due to Each} \\ \text{Supplier Quality Problem}}}{\text{Total Purchase Value from Each Supplier}}$$

N VALUE

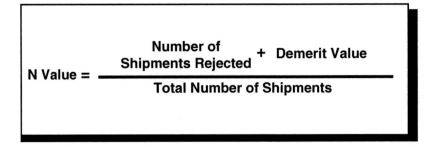

$$N\text{ Value} = \frac{\substack{\text{Number of} \\ \text{Shipments Rejected}} + \text{Demerit Value}}{\text{Total Number of Shipments}}$$

SUPPLY MANAGEMENT MEASUREMENTS

CHAPTER SIX

We would like to introduce this chapter by demonstrating how one organization views supply management and the relationship between customers and suppliers. ABB (Asea Brown Boveri) recently held an International Supply Management Conference in Zurich, Switzerland at which we gave a presentation. During this conference, ABB invited its suppliers to an introduction of their Supply Management program. All Supply Management programs require written policy statements on quality as well as commitments and expectations. They serve as an excellent basis for introducing certification candidates to the Supply Management process.

Mission Statement

ABB's mission is to be the leader in delivering quality products and services for power generation, transmission and distribution, industrial processes, mass transit, and environmental control that meet the needs and requirements of their customers and contribute to their success.

To ensure customer satisfaction, ABB provides value-added, integrated solutions that are driven by superior technology and performance. ABB's employees are committed to leadership standards in applying the

---

company's unique combination of experience and global resources to meeting societal goals for sustainable growth and clean energy.

The key is to provide each supplier with a knowledge of your mission and expectations. There should be no surprises in the supply base.

It is extremely important to solicit input from suppliers on how they can become a better customer. The supplier certification process includes a two-way constructive discussion on how ABB and its suppliers can consistently meet or exceed ABB and its customer requirements and expectations the first time and every time. Suppliers who have served well over the years will be afforded an opportunity to participate in a Supplier Certification Program. However, the intention is to reduce the supply base over time, with the objective to work with a number of highly qualified suppliers.

Supplier Certification Policy

The company is committed to provide to its customers products and services which will meet or exceed customer requirements. ABB is further committed to be a highly competitive producer, provide superior service to its customers and maintain excellence in technology and quality. In order to achieve these goals, the goods and services that it *purchases* must consistently meet or exceed these criteria.

SUPPLY MANAGEMENT MEASUREMENT CRITERIA

Suppliers as Partners

- Actual vs. planned total costs

- Quoted lead time vs. actual delivery time

- Number of new agreements reached

- Number of single sources developed

- Number of suppliers reduced

- Number of parts consolidated

- Number of on-time deliveries per order per buyer

- Number of past due orders per supplier

- Total cost savings

NUMBER OF SUPPLIERS

Purpose:　　　　This measurement should show the number of suppliers currently being utilized. Each represents a cost to source, prepare a PO for, certify, process invoices and pay. The goal is to reduce the number of suppliers and thus reduce cost.

Responsibility:　Purchasing should be responsible for this measurement. But, all functions of the company, including manufacturing, engineering, administration and management, should participate in the reduction.

Reporting:　　　The measurement should be reflected in graphs and reports. Graphs should emphasize numbers and dollars.

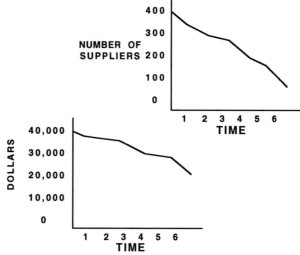

Calculation of Dollars:

Dollars = processing cost x # of suppliers

Processing cost = time x material
$120 = 40 x $3

Processing time (labor) = sourcing + P.O. + receiver + updating inventory + invoice + voucher + check + reconciliation + changes (on all of the above)

$40 = $8/hr. x 5 hrs.

Materials = all internal and external documents used to conduct business with suppliers

AVAILABILITY

$$\text{Availability} = \frac{\text{Number of times when goods were available from the supplier when ordering}}{\text{Number of orders placed with the supplier}}$$

RATIO OF REJECTION

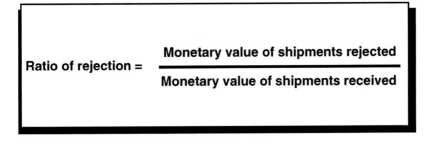

$$\text{Ratio of rejection} = \frac{\text{Monetary value of shipments rejected}}{\text{Monetary value of shipments received}}$$

NUMBER OF SUPPLIERS CERTIFIED

Purpose: Measurement should reflect the company's activity toward certification of suppliers. In the beginning stages, the measurement could reflect the number of suppliers involved in the certification process.

Responsibility: All functions involved with the process of Supplier Certification should be concerned with this measurement. Management, purchasing, manufacturing, quality, engineering and finance should have responsibility for accelerating this measurement.

Reporting: This measurement should be depicted in a graph maintained and displayed by the certification team.

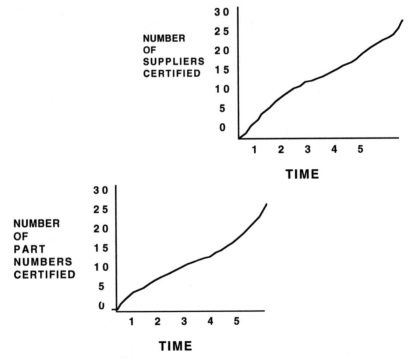

DELIVERY PERFORMANCE

CHAPTER SEVEN

Supplier delivery performance has a direct correlation to a number of other critical performance measurements, such as schedule attainment, customer deliveries, inventory planning, and cash flow consideration. It is for this reason that supplier delivery performance is considered a vital indicator, requiring continuous monitoring and corrective action. In order to accurately and fairly develop a purchasing supplier delivery performance history, a "firm" definition of the required delivery date must be established. Generally, this date is within supplier stated lead times or promise dates and meets the purchaser's required delivery date.

In some cases, you may develop a period of flexibility for on-time delivery, such as one to two days on either side of the delivery date. However, with World Class manufacturing techniques as an ever increasing fact of life, specific delivery dates become critical.

Source: Materials

 ## Supplier Delivery Performance Measurement Criteria

The following are viable measurement criteria in the area of purchasing/supplier delivery performance:

- **Actual total purchase orders or individual line items measured on actual delivery date against scheduled/due date.**

- **Actual dollars ($) of purchased receipts against plan.**

- **Actual purchase order quantities against schedule release quantities.**

- **Actual quantities received against purchase order quantities, taking into account company policy with respect to over- or undershipments.**

- **Line item delivery time compared to actual delivery time.**

ON-TIME DELIVERY

What percentage of supplier deliveries are on time? ___%

**How is on-time delivery measured to the delivery date?
+/- __ hours +/- __ one day +/- __ five days __other (explain)**

On-time delivery compares the actual receipt date to the supplier's committed delivery date based on shop need. This is obviously an important measurement since World Class manufacturing relies on just-in-time delivery from suppliers. Remember, however, that overshipments and early delivery is just as costly as late delivery. If you're receiving parts two or three days ahead of schedule, inventory will rise. The higher the percentage of suppliers delivering on-time and the smaller your delivery window, the closer you come to being a World Class company. This is a measurement which needs to be calculated for delivery as a whole and for each individual supplier in order to gain improvement.

It is necessary for you to first determine what the on-time delivery baseline is. It could be:

1) **the requested Purchase Order date,**
2) **the supplier's acknowledged date,**

3) the supplier's lead time translated into a delivery date,
4) the supplier's ready date if the FOB point is the supplier's dock, or
5) FOB your dock.

Whatever definition you choose, make sure that you and your supplier both have agreed to it and understand it. We recommend that you monitor both the acknowledged date as your baseline as well as your requested date for reference. The difference between them is the lead time. Then, both you and the supplier can work to reduce the lead time in order to get true on-time delivery.

EARLY DELIVERY

Early delivery = ($ amount of inventory that was early) x (9%/360) x (# of days early) + (# of days early) x (daily inventory carrying cost)

LATE DELIVERY

Late delivery = ($ amount of inventory that was late) x (9%/360) x (# of days late) + (# of days late) x (daily inventory carrying cost)

OVERSHIPMENTS

Overshipments = ($ of overshipments) x (inventory carrying cost)

$ of overshipments = (% of time overship) x ($ value of inventory)

FROM SHIP-TO-STOCK TO SHIP-TO-WIP

The point of JIT delivery, production, inventory is to adjust from the philosophy of "ship-to-stock" to the philosophy of "ship-to-WIP." Let's pretend the supplier's truck is outside our door. What do we do now?

First of all, you may wonder just how it got to your door. Whose responsibility is that? In a World Class environment, transportation may fall under the umbrella of Purchasing. First, delivery schedules are now part of the negotiations which lead to an agreement. Second, transportation is vital to the operation of your plant. Third, transportation depends upon good relations with suppliers and transportation companies. These relations are supported by buyer/planners who know your company's material requirements and production schedules so they are able to communicate procurement schedules to suppliers.

Long-term objectives are to send the parts directly to the work station on the production line where they will be used. "Ship-to-WIP" is the movement of zero-defect material directly to the work station on the production line where it is needed, at just the time it is needed, in the quantity it is needed.

There are six ship-to-WIP guidelines for you to follow:

1.   **Evaluate supplier's ability to provide total quality control and delivery performance.**

2.   **Obtain commitment of JIT delivery and TQC product from supplier's management.**

3.   **Conduct a complete and detailed quality survey of supplier.**

4.   **Develop a strategy to incorporate total quality control and on-time delivery performance, based on commodity.**

5.   **Review and modify the plan with suppliers and listen carefully to their suggestions.**

6.   **Put the plan into action. Audit and maintain it through a sound supplier relationship.**

**What percentage of your procured material is shipped directly to Work-In-Process? _____%
To stock? _____%**

Why is this a critical measurement of Supplier Partnerships?

LEAD TIME

The measurement of lead time often reveals that over half of lead time is taken up by queues. We can greatly reduce queue time by shipping directly to the line and even eliminate queues outright in a true World Class environment.

Couple queue reduction with set-up reduction and you can readily see that you don't have to accept lead times as unchangeable. Purchasing, by monitoring progress on supplier set-up and queue reduction, plays a large role in shortening lead times. Shorter lead times lead to a higher inventory turnover rate and a greater return on assets.

What percentage of material is actually being processed as opposed to sitting in queue? ___%

Describe your work center queues:
Nonexistent __ Low (minutes) __ Moderate (hours) __ High (days) __ Very High (weeks) __

LEAD TIME OBJECTIVES

Lead time represents a costly utilization of a wide variety of company resources. Its reduction is both a vital cost of quality and cost reduction opportunity. The following are the objectives of a lead time reduction process at a World Class company:

REDUCE OR ELIMINATE SET-UP
Set-up is a nonproductive, income-using element of lead time. It impedes the response by a supplier to customer requirements and negatively impacts line and machine efficiency.

IMPROVE MOVE TIME
Material handling is a nonproductive use of resources. The goal is reduce the quantity of material moved and thus simplify material handling. We like to calculate touch points.

MATCH LOT SIZES TO CUSTOMER DEMAND
Reductions in lead time allow you to approach a lot size of one part. In essence, the goal is to produce on time exactly what the customer orders.

TIME TO MARKET
Time to market and throughput reductions accelerate production flow which results in lower inventory carrying costs, lower cost of quality and more floor space.

TRANSPORTATION COSTS

This measurement will make you look more closely at what it costs you to receive material and to ship your product. It will force you to ask yourself the following types of questions:

- **What is the cost of air freight vs. ground transportation?**
  $_____ vs. $_____
- **What is the cost of shipping by boat from overseas suppliers?**
  $_____

- **What percentage of your freight is delivered or shipped at priority levels?**

- **What percentage of the price of purchased material is inbound freight? _____%**

- **What percentage of sales is outbound freight? _____%**

The point, obviously, is to reduce your costs and find the most economical method of transportation.

PRIORITY FREIGHT COST

Priority freight cost = Delta difference between premium freight cost vs. surface freight cost

AIR FREIGHT COST

Air freight cost = Delta difference between air freight cost vs. surface freight cost

SURFACE FREIGHT COST

Surface freight cost = Dollars charged for surface freight priced as less than truck load (LTL) or truck load for that commodity code

EARLY SHIPMENT
INVENTORY ANALYSIS

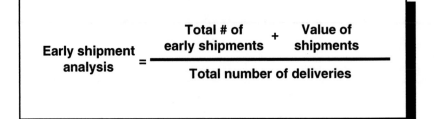

$$\text{Early shipment analysis} = \frac{\text{Total \# of early shipments} + \text{Value of shipments}}{\text{Total number of deliveries}}$$

SUPPLIER
EXPEDITING SUMMARY

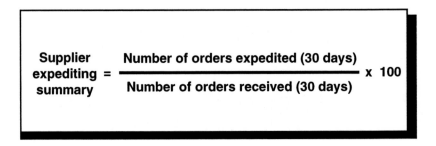

$$\text{Supplier expediting summary} = \frac{\text{Number of orders expedited (30 days)}}{\text{Number of orders received (30 days)}} \times 100$$

COST MEASUREMENTS

CHAPTER EIGHT

Sharing cost information provides mutual benefits for both suppliers and customers. It helps build commitment to long-term supplier relationships which protect supplier profitability while assuring the customer of acceptable costs. The supplier should be actively involved in cost control programs and should be able to demonstrate that it is engaged in the following activities:

- To what degree can the supplier demonstrate that they are actively involved in programs to control and reduce costs in the areas of waste reduction, supplier cost control, productivity improvement, efficiency improvement, and technological advancement?

- To what extent does the supplier set cost standards against which operations can be meaningfully and usefully measured and to what extent do they mirror the usage, efficiency, productivity and other quality and control measures utilized in the production process?

- To what extent are standard and other costs allocated appropriately to the supplier's product purchased by the customer?

- To what extent does the supplier's Accounting staff interact with Operating staff? Is reporting of results frequent and useful?

- To what extent is the supplier familiar with the cost of quality?

- To what degree do the supplier's customers benefit from the results of cost control measures?

- To what extent does the supplier control lead-time costs?

- To what extent does the supplier effectively control raw material, intermediate material and finished goods inventories?

- To what extent is the supplier willing and able to provide the components of cost?

COST OF
PURCHASE ORDER

$$\text{Cost of purchase order} = \frac{\text{Administrative costs + processing + all touch points + overhead}}{\text{Number of orders placed}}$$

COST PER SUPPLIER IN DATABASE

Cost per supplier in database $=$ $\dfrac{\text{(Estimated time to process PO) + (estimated time to pay invoice) + (incoming inspection) x (\# of POs per year)}}{\text{Number of suppliers in database}}$

PURCHASE COST RATIO

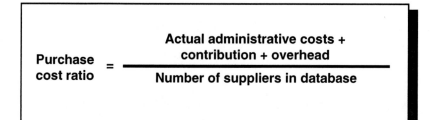

Purchase cost ratio $=$ $\dfrac{\text{Actual administrative costs + contribution + overhead}}{\text{Number of suppliers in database}}$

COST AVOIDANCE RATIO

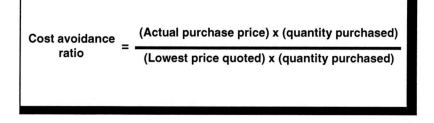

Cost avoidance ratio $=$ $\dfrac{\text{(Actual purchase price) x (quantity purchased)}}{\text{(Lowest price quoted) x (quantity purchased)}}$

COST REDUCTION

Cost reduction = $\dfrac{\text{Current purchase price}}{\text{Prior standard price}}$

COST SAVINGS RATIO

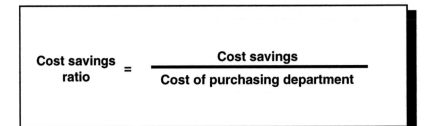

Cost savings ratio = $\dfrac{\text{Cost savings}}{\text{Cost of purchasing department}}$

RATIO OF PRICE DIFFERENCE

Ratio of price difference = $\dfrac{\text{Actual price}}{\text{Planned price}}$

TOTAL PRICE DIFFERENCE

Total price
difference   = (Actual price − planned price) x (quantity purchased)

ACQUISITION COST

Acquisition
    cost   = R + P + I + S + T + L + IS + SF + E

Note: Company must calculate values for each function or element listed below.

R = Receiving cost
P = PO processing cost
I   = Inspection test cost
S = Staffing cost
T = Transit cost
L = Lead time
IS = Information system
SF = Space (square footage)
E = Education and training

SUPPLIER FINANCIAL EVALUATION

CHAPTER NINE

Preference will be given to suppliers who can demonstrate that they are financially secure and are effectively using assets to generate profits, invest in research and development, and manage their business. These are the types of suppliers you want to make into partners. Ask yourself this question with each supplier: What is the financial stability of the supplier as determined by the following financial ratios?

Quick Ratio: **(Cash + Accounts Receivable)/Current Liabilities**

Shows the amount of available liquid assets to cover current debt.

Current Ratio: **Current Assets/Current Liabilities**

Measures a supplier's margin of safety to cover reductions in current assets.

Current Liabilities
to Net Worth: Current Liabilities/Net Worth

Contrasts the year's amount due to creditors with funds invested by owners.

Total Liabilities
to Net Worth: Total Liabilities/Net Worth

Contrasts total indebtedness to funds invested by owners.

Fixed Assets
to Net Worth: Fixed Assets/Net Worth

A smaller ratio is generally desired.

Collection Period: Accounts Receivable x 360/Sales

Reflects the average number of days it takes to collect a receivable.

Inventory Turnover: Sales/Inventory

Shows how quickly supplies and material flows through the organization.

Accounts Payable
to Sales: Accounts Payable/Sales

Measures how much of supplier's money is being used to generate sales.

Return on Sales
(Profit Margin):   Net Profit after Taxes/Sales

Measures efficiency of organization.

Return on Assets: Net Profit after Taxes/Total Assets

A key indicator of profitability for the organization.

Return on Net Worth
(Return on Equity):   Net Profit after Taxes/Net Worth

Measures the ability of the supplier to realize an adequate return on capital.

ADMINISTRATIVE
MEASUREMENTS

CHAPTER TEN

The objective and goal for a company is to work with suppliers who embrace the continuous improvement mindset and who adopt a commitment, dedication and culture which is conducive to change. These qualities will significantly simplify the attainment of World Class status.

In reviewing the approach of many companies, we often find a lack of leadership, planning and direction in their purchasing performance measurements. Many companies feel that when they educate the workers the responsibility for the program's success has passed from management to direct labor. These same companies, however, fail to realize that constant monitoring is crucial to the World Class process.

Attaining World Class status requires support, not criticism, and the total endorsement of the program by management within the company. In order to do this, administrative measurement must be developed early in the program. The suggestions in this section are intended to help you track your attainment of excellence in this area.

BUYER'S SERVICE LEVEL

$$\text{Buyer's service level} = \frac{\text{Out of stocks}}{\text{Potential total sales}} \times 100$$

CURRENT MONTH EXPENSE VARIANCE

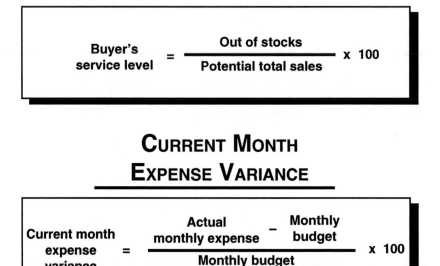

$$\text{Current month expense variance} = \frac{\text{Actual monthly expense} - \text{Monthly budget}}{\text{Monthly budget}} \times 100$$

PURCHASING WORKLOAD

$$\text{Purchasing workload standard} = \frac{\text{Number of hours}}{\text{Document}}$$

NUMBER OF DOCUMENTS/WEEK

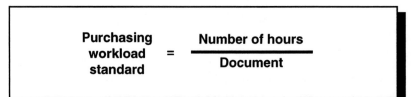

$$\text{Number of documents/ week} = \frac{\text{Number of hours per week per buying activity}}{\text{Standard}}$$

NUMBER OF DOCUMENTS
PER YEAR PER BUYER

Number of
documents
per year per = (Number of documents per week) x (49 weeks per year)
buyer

PLANNED NUMBER
OF BUYERS

$$\text{Planned number of buyers} = \frac{\text{Projected workload per year}}{\text{Number of documents per year per buyer}}$$

PRODUCT FLOW

$$\text{Critical factor} = \frac{\text{Number of urgent orders}}{\text{Total number of orders placed}}$$

$$\text{Reliability factor} = \frac{\text{Number of orders delivered on date planned}}{\text{Total number of orders placed}}$$

INPUT RATIO

$$\text{Input ratio} \ = \ \frac{\text{Number of requisitions received}}{\text{Number of orders placed}}$$

YEAR TO DATE EXPENSE VARIANCE

$$\begin{array}{l}\text{Year to date} \\ \text{expense} \ = \\ \text{variance}\end{array} \ \frac{(\text{Actual YTD expense}) \ - \ (\text{YTD budget})}{\text{YTD budget}} \ \text{x} \ 100$$

ADDITIONAL MEASUREMENTS

CHAPTER ELEVEN

We measure performance in order to be predictable, so that we know where we have been, where we are and where we are going. In short, so we don't make the same mistake twice. Of course, it is possible to measure the wrong items, to measure after the fact and to measure meaningless quantities. The problem with the old yardsticks of performance measurements is that they are guilty of misrepresentations of actual sales, forecasts, schedules and productivity because they use a reactive, rather than a proactive scale.

Today's purchasing professionals must use new yardsticks which collect data and look at it over a period of time. Then, when it is time to make a decision, you will be able to compare actual data against predicted performance. This gives you the opportunity to take corrective action.

PURCHASE ORDER CHANGES

Purpose: Allows the company to track the number of changes to Purchase Orders and analyze the reasons for the changes. The cost to make changes needs to be calculated in order to emphasize the need to improve.

Responsibility: Responsibility for this measurement should be with the Purchasing department. However, the company needs to track the causes of the changes back to the function creating the requisition and changes.

Reporting: This measurement should be displayed in graphs which reflect the number of changes and the costs.

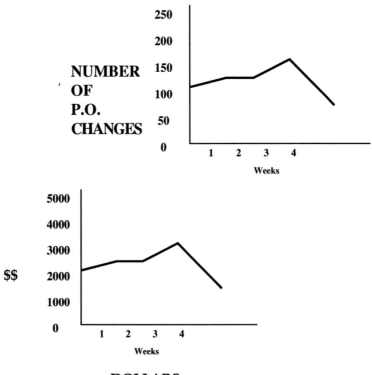

Calculation of dollars:

Dollars per week = Processing cost x number of changes
$7,500   = $75   x   100

Processing cost = Time to process x rate
$75   =   3 hours   x $25

Time to process = Analysis + preparing P.O. + receiving
+ inspection + updating records

Rate = Average dollar of functions impacted

RECEIPTS TO INVENTORY/WIP

Purpose: This measurement represents the company's efforts in moving toward the delivery of materials directly to work-in-process instead of inventory. This measurement should promote the analysis of why materials are not allowed to be delivered directly to the floor.

Responsibility: The buyer/planner must be responsible for maintaining the measurement and the activities toward continuous improvements.

Reporting: A measurement graph should reflect the percent relationship between materials going into inventory versus directly to their destinations. The cost of the intermediate stops before getting to the floor should also be calculated and reported.

Calculation of dollars (graphs on following page):

Dollars = Labor (Price x carrying cost % x days)
$30,000 = 20.00 ($20,000 x 25% x 3)

Labor = Average labor dollars to receive + count + inspect + stock

Price = Material dollars cost

Carrying cost % = Computed carrying cost % of inventory per day

Days = Days to get to the floor

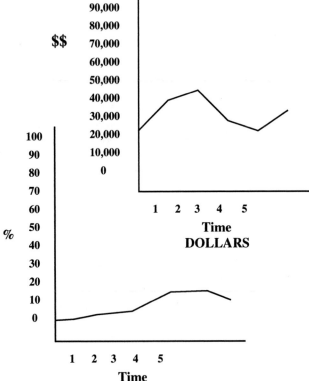

DOLLARS

MATERIAL RECEIPTS DELIVERED
TO FLOOR PERCENTAGE

FORECASTING ACCURACY

What percentage of the time does your forecast reflect actual sales levels? ___%

Planning for production and procurement schedules depends on short-term, accurate forecasting. The way to measure accuracy is to measure how large or small the error is between the forecast and reality.

DATA ACCURACY

> **What is the level of data accuracy (by area; e.g. Bill of Material, Routing, Inventory) ___%**

Data accuracy is an "up-front" consideration. We exist in a company environment where change is the only certainty. It is imperative that the information which we use in planning is up-to-date, as close to a real-time environment as is possible. You simply can't forecast, plan, schedule or produce without the most basic of raw materials — accurate information.

MATERIAL HANDLING

Purpose:　　　The movement of materials through the company is nonproductive and therefore waste. Movement in and out of inventory, from one operation to another and from plant to warehouse needs to be identified, analyzed and then eliminated.

Responsibility:　　Each function that deals with materials should ask itself how material arrives and where the next receiving area is. These functions need to take responsibility for finding ways to reduce the effort and the time it takes to move material through the com-pany. This measurement should include nonmaterial moves such as engineering change orders, invoices, production schedules and packing slips.

Reporting:　　Measurements should be represented on a graph showing the time involved in moving something.

• How much material handling is required to support production?
　　　None ___ Minimal ___ Moderate ___ High ___

• Labor hours and dollars utilized for material handling.___ **hours/$___**

• Number of material handling services (forklifts) and operations?_____

• Travel distance, by operation, required in handling material?_____

LACK OF COMPETITION

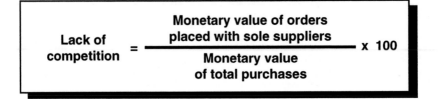

$$\text{Lack of competition} = \frac{\text{Monetary value of orders placed with sole suppliers}}{\text{Monetary value of total purchases}} \times 100$$

MEASURING
CUSTOMS, DUTY, AND FREIGHT

$$\text{Customs, duty, and freight} = \frac{\text{Percentage of duties collected associated with international business}}{\text{Total business activity}}$$

NUMBER OF LINE ITEMS ISSUED

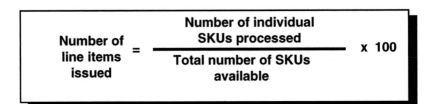

$$\text{Number of line items issued} = \frac{\text{Number of individual SKUs processed}}{\text{Total number of SKUs available}} \times 100$$

PERCENTAGE OF
LOCAL BUSINESS ACTIVITY

$$\text{Percentage of local business activity} = \frac{\text{Total number of local businesses}}{\text{Total supplier base}} \times 100$$

MINORITY BUSINESS ACTIVITY

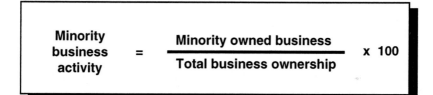

$$\text{Minority business activity} = \frac{\text{Minority owned business}}{\text{Total business ownership}} \times 100$$

WOMAN OWNED BUSINESS

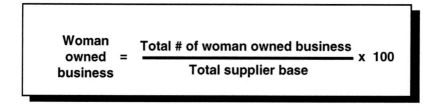

$$\text{Woman owned business} = \frac{\text{Total \# of woman owned business}}{\text{Total supplier base}} \times 100$$

PURCHASING
PERFORMANCE
GRID

CHAPTER TWELVE

You have seen numerous examples of measurements in this book. Measuring a company's success and present position provides both a "snapshot" in time and a vehicle for improvement. We have tried to provide you with the most comprehensive list of purchasing measurements of which we know. This includes indices, formulas and ratios. We have included those key measurements, which if not measured, will result in failure on your journey to World Class excellence.

The challenge in purchasing performance measurement is to make sense from the mass of information which is collected. The Business Performance Grid on the following pages should serve as a guide in helping you establish an overall measurement process.

You must be sure that all your purchasing measurements are interrelated for the achievement of World Class status. The key is to establish a benchmark today with goals and objectives which must be accomplished. Once a base is established, you should measure and monitor your progress toward the goal.

STEP 1

By period, sum the performance figures for the nine performance categories and enter total in "raw total" block of the Purchasing Performance Grid. The typical maximum score, by category entry, is 100 (the maximum total score is 900).

Note: All nine categories must be measured in order to present a true "closed loop" picture of business performance.

STEP 2

Divide "raw total" by nine and enter figure in "average %" block.

STEP 3

Determine classification utilizing the following table and enter in the "classification" block.

> A = 90% PLUS
> B = 80 - 89%
> C = 70 - 79%
> D = 60 - 69%

Note: A particular performance classification must be monitored for a minimum of three consecutive periods in order to "certify" that level of performance.

STEP 4

Utilize the "notations" column to reference supporting data, which details reasons for exceptional and/or unsatisfactory performances.

On Page 89, there is a blank form for your use.

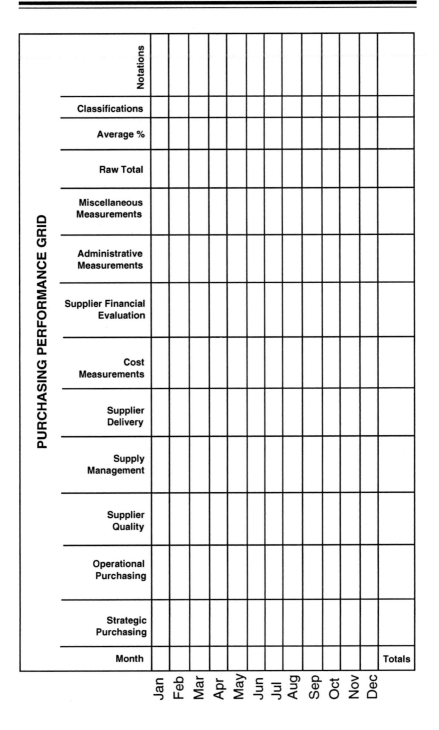

PURCHASING MANAGERS' INDEX

A useful tool for purchasing professionals is printed monthly in the trade journal, *NAPM Insights*. The National Association for Purchasing Management has formed a Business Survey Committee whose task it is to collect and analyze data on the status of the economy. The most widely known of its measurements is the Purchasing Managers' Index (PMI). The PMI tracks both the manufacturing and overall economies and indicates whether they are declining or expanding. The magazine also reports on the overall direction of local economies around the country.

Besides these general indicators, *NAPM Insights* also reports on 10 other areas of interest to purchasing professionals:

- **Production**

- **New Orders**

- **Backlog of Orders**

- **Supplier Deliveries**

- **Inventory**

- **Employment**

- **Prices**

- **New Export Orders**

- **Imports**

MANAGEMENT
SUPPORT
■CHAPTER THIRTEEN■

Top management must commit its support to the change process and the creation of a company culture which fosters responsibility, authority, vision and accountability at the lowest level. Management must accept answers which may be difficult to hear. Management commitment means creating an environment where performance measurement is the norm. If you want to improve purchasing and supplier performance, you must measure progress. This will provide you with the means to see where you have been, where you want to be and how fast you are getting there. Unless you track your progress, it is easy to lose sight of your accomplishments and thus lose the momentum needed to keep the process moving forward. Performance measurements provide proof of success and failure, an honest evaluation of the efforts you have made.

On the following page are the major commitments top management needs to make.

TOP MANAGEMENT REQUIREMENTS

	YES	NO
• Establish supply management goals and objectives which can be reached.	___	___
• Use patience and persistence in working with suppliers.	___	___
• Develop a trust with internal/external suppliers and customers. (Partnership)	___	___
• Improve communications with suppliers. (Partnership)	___	___
• Delegate responsibility, authority, vision and accountability to the purchasing professional.	___	___
• Adopt a Six Sigma approach. (Zero defects)	___	___
• Allocate/authorize financial support.	___	___
• Devote resources to project teams. (Employee involvement and capital)	___	___
• Risk short-term operational results for long-term improvements. (Total Cost)	___	___
• Foster communication and cooperation. (Team Building)	___	___

	YES	NO
• Review, monitor, document and measure. (Performance measurements)	____	____
• Support an ongoing training and education program for suppliers. (Continuous Improvement Process)	____	____
• Foster a "no waiver" environment and attitude in processes and specifications. (Fitness for Use)	____	____
• Develop a purchasing reward mechanism for achievements. (Employee Involvement)	____	____

EDUCATION
AND
TRAINING
MEASUREMENT

- Has top management, the project team and key personnel attended external training classes?

- Have money, time and resources been allocated? Has internal education been established?

- Has internal education been planned and employed with capable outside instruction and applicable materials?

- Has an ongoing supply management education program been established?

- Are suppliers included in your internal education and training?

Additional Purchasing Resources
from PT Publications, Inc.
3109 45th Street, Suite 100
West Palm Beach, FL 33407

PROFESSIONAL TEXTBOOKS

MADE IN AMERICA: *The Total Business Concept*
Peter L. Grieco, Jr. and Michael W. Gozzo

> Full of case studies, charts, tables, tactics and strategies. *302 pages*

JUST-IN-TIME PURCHASING: *In Pursuit of Excellence*
Peter L. Grieco, Jr., Michael W. Gozzo and Jerry W. Claunch

> "...must reading for purchasers and every level of management that are just starting or intending to pursue JIT." —
> **Electronic Buyers News**. *199 pages*

SUPPLIER CERTIFICATION II: *A Handbook for*
Achieving Excellence through Continuous Improvement
Peter L. Grieco, Jr.

> Over 20,000 copies sold worldwide. Most effective when used with our *Supply Management Toolbox*. *549 pages*

BEHIND BARS: *Bar Coding Principles and Applications*
Peter L. Grieco, Jr., Michael W. Gozzo and C.J. (Chip) Long

> Find out how bar coding can work for you. *244 pages*

SET-UP REDUCTION: *Saving Dollars with Common Sense*
Jerry W. Claunch and Philip D. Stang

> Step-by-step guide to implementing and institutionalizing set-up reduction in your company. Save money now! *309 pages*

WORLD CLASS: *Measuring Its Achievement*
Peter L. Grieco, Jr.

> "The best holistic measurement book around." — Carl Cooper, Senior Applications Consultant for Motorola University. *287 pages*

THE WORLD OF NEGOTIATIONS: *Never Being a Loser*
Peter L. Grieco, Jr. and Paul G. Hine

> How to master the art of world class negotiations. *242 pages*

PEOPLE EMPOWERMENT: *Achieving Success from Involvement*
Michael W. Gozzo and Wayne L. Douchkoff

> Learn how and why to empower your employees so as to net the most success from their involvement. *288 pages*

ACTIVITY BASED COSTING: *The Key to World Class Performance*
Peter L. Grieco, Jr. and Mel Pilachowski

> Develop and implement a costing system which provides information to make your company more efficient and profitable. *243 pages*

SUPPLY MANAGEMENT TOOLBOX: *How to Manage Your Suppliers*
Peter L. Grieco, Jr.

> The companion book to *Supplier Certification II*. All the forms and charts you need to get your process up and running. *344 pages*

POWER PURCHASING: *Supply Management in the 21st Century*
Peter L. Grieco, Jr. and Carl R. Cooper

> A practical guide for companies who want to understand the paradigm shift in Purchasing. *204 pages*

GLOSSARY OF KEY PURCHASING TERMS, ACRONYMS, AND FORMULAS
PT Publications

> The latest terms in the field of purchasing are explained and detailed.

VIDEO EDUCATION SERIES

SUPPLIER CERTIFICATION: *The Path to Excellence*

A nine-tape series on World Class Supplier Based Management. The best explanation in its field.

AUDIO PROFESSIONAL EDUCATION TAPES

THE WORLD OF NEGOTIATIONS: *How to Win Every Time*

A leading edge audio tape on developing a negotiating strategy based on Total Cost, Total Quality Control, Just-In-Time and World Class relationships. Focus is on a company-wide strategy. Nobody else has a tape like this.

> To find out more about our extensive offerings,
> give us a call at 1-800-272-4335.

A

Accounts payable to sales 74
Acquisition cost 11, 71
Administrative measurements 75-78
Availability 57

B

Baseline 1, 4
Benchmarking 1, 9
Bill of Material (BOM) 23
Business planning 14
Buyer's service level 76

C

Capacity Requirements Plan (CRP) 20
"Cloning" 4
Collection period 74
Competition 84
Continuous Improvement Process (CIP) 1-2
Cooperation 38
Corrective action 9
Cost measurements 67-71
Cost of inspection 51
Cost of procurement 11
Cost of receiving 51
Cost performance 37
Current liabilities to net worth 74
Current month expense variance 76
Current ratio 73
Customer service 24
Customs, duty and freight 84
Cycle count 21

D

E

F

G

I

J

L

M

R

Ratio of price difference 70
Ratio of rejection 57
Receipts to inventory/WIP 81
Return On Assets (ROA) 32, 74
Return On Investment (ROI) 14
Return On Net Assets (RONA) 14
Return on net worth 74
Return on sales 74
Rework and scrap 49
RTV 51

S

Sales 15
Ship-to-stock to ship-to-WIP 62
Shop floor 50
Statistical Process Control (SPC) 50
Strategic procurement planning 18
Supplier certification 34, 54
Supplier Parts Per Million (SPPM) 48
Supplier performance rating 33-39
Supplier quality cost index 52
Supplier Quality Rating (SQR) 47
Suppliers as partners 55
Supply management measurements 53-58

T

Thriving on Chaos 25
Throughput 30
Total Business Concept (TBC) 8
Total liabilities to net worth 74
Transportation costs 65

W

Woman owned business 85

Y

Year-to-date expense variance 78